SPEAK UP!
CONFRONTING DISCRIMINATION IN YOUR DAILY LIFE

CONFRONTING RACISM

MARYELLEN LO BOSCO

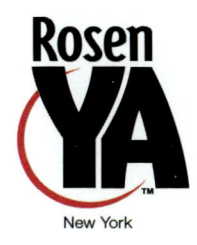

Rosen YA
New York

Published in 2018 by The Rosen Publishing Group, Inc.
29 East 21st Street, New York, NY 10010

Copyright © 2018 by The Rosen Publishing Group, Inc.

First Edition

All rights reserved. No part of this book may be reproduced in any form without permission in writing from the publisher, except by a reviewer.

Library of Congress Cataloging-in-Publication Data

Names: Lo Bosco, Maryellen, author.
Title: Confronting racism / Maryellen Lo Bosco.
Description: New York, NY: Rosen Publishing Group, Inc., 2018. | Series: Speak up! Confronting discrimination in your daily life | Includes bibliographical references and index. | Audience: Grades 7–12.
Identifiers: LCCN 2017022754| ISBN 9781538381786 (library bound) | ISBN 9781538381762 (pbk.) | ISBN 9781538381779 (6 pack)
Subjects: LCSH: Race discrimination—United States—Juvenile literature. | Racism—United States—Juvenile literature. | United States—Race relations—Juvenile literature.
Classification: LCC E184.A1 B67 2018 | DDC 305.800973—dc23
LC record available at https://lccn.loc.gov/2017022754

Manufactured in the United States of America

CONTENTS

INTRODUCTION   4

CHAPTER ONE
A BRIEF HISTORY OF RACISM   8

CHAPTER TWO
THE STRUGGLE FOR CIVIL RIGHTS AND RACIAL EQUALITY IN THE UNITED STATES   15

CHAPTER THREE
LEGAL PROTECTIONS AGAINST RACIAL DISCRIMINATION   23

CHAPTER FOUR
SPOTTING AND ADDRESSING OVERT RACIAL DISCRIMINATION   33

CHAPTER FIVE
SPOTTING AND ADDRESSING COVERT DISCRIMINATION IN THE CLASSROOM   40

CHAPTER SIX
STAYING HEALTHY IN A WORLD THAT IS NOT POSTRACIAL   48

GLOSSARY   54
FOR MORE INFORMATION   56
FOR FURTHER READING   59
BIBLIOGRAPHY   60
INDEX   62

INTRODUCTION

Racism—or, the hatred and mistreatment of one race by another—is an age-old problem and a phenomenon that has occurred in different guises, in many cultures the world over, back to ancient history. One form of racism is xenophobia, which is the fear and hatred of foreigners or strangers.

According to evolutionary biologists, xenophobia has its origin in the behavior of territorial males. Aggression toward strangers has been observed in chimpanzees, one of two of our closest primate relatives. The other—bonobos—resolve conflicts with rival groups through promiscuous sexual behavior. Human beings are neither chimps nor bonobos, and when it comes to xenophobia or racism, human children do not fear foreigners or recognize physical differences until they have been taught to do so.

Science, in the form of the Human Genome Project, has taught us that there is no such thing as race from the standpoint of biology, because there is so little difference in DNA between one human being and another. Scientists have reasoned that *homo sapiens sapiens*—modern humans—came from a small and undiversified cohort of ancestors who left Africa about sixty thousand years ago to populate the planet. And here we are.

While race may not be founded in scientific fact, it is real from a social and cultural perspective—and in

INTRODUCTION | 5

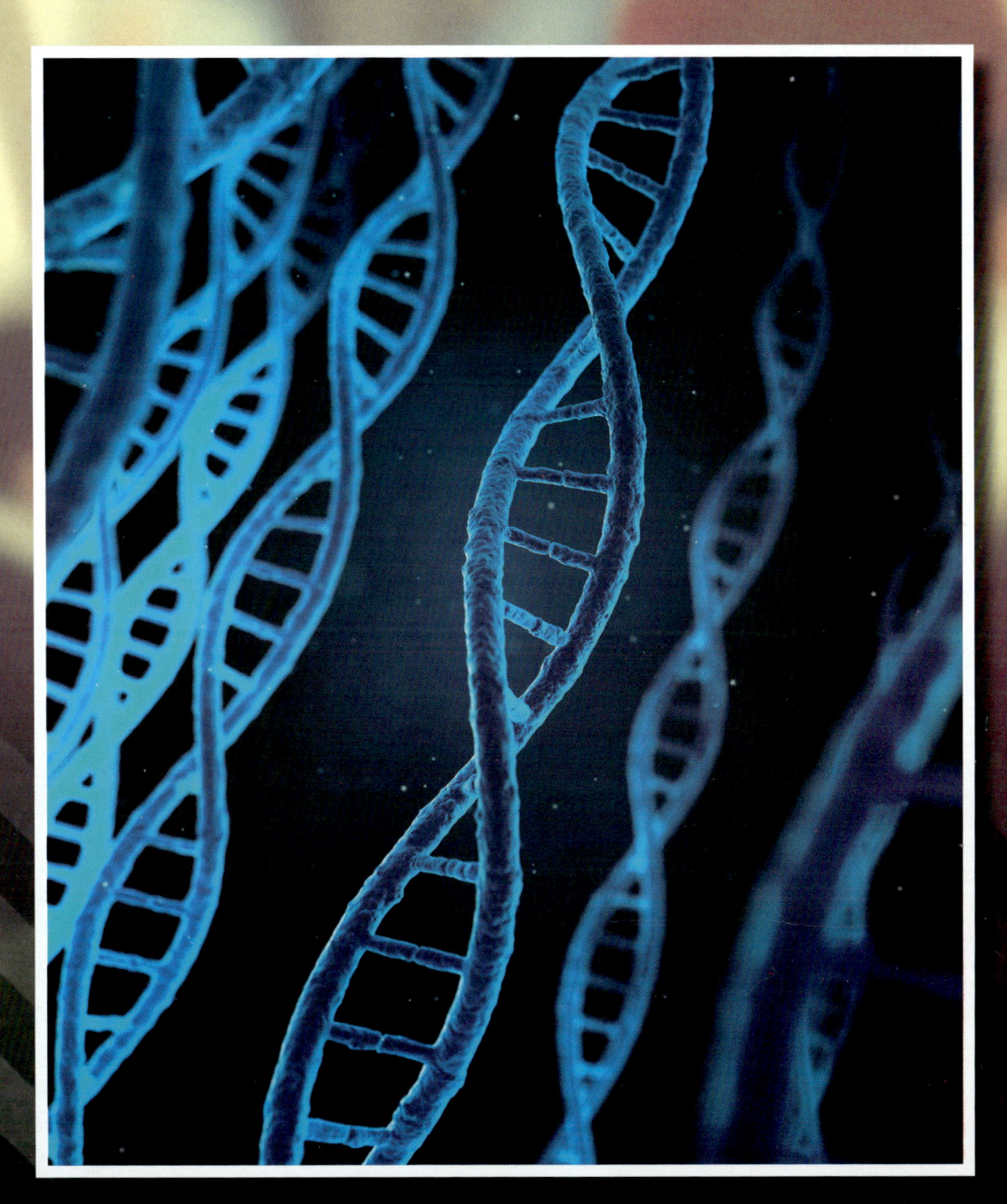

Human beings are among the least diverse of species. Current evolutionary theory holds that the planet was populated by a

turn, *racism* is very real. In the United States, racism continues to be a pervasive and difficult problem and one that is inextricably woven into our history. From America's beginnings in 1619, Europeans brought African slaves to these shores to use mostly as agricultural laborers; as the country grew, so did the slave population. Although slavery was not new in the world, America's linkage of slavery and racism was particularly pernicious. Americans concluded that it was permissible to hold black people in bondage because they were not "human" in the way that white people were. This rationalization for slavery became necessary

Harriet Tubman (*far left*) was a resistance fighter and key figure in the Underground Railroad, a network of abolitionists who helped slaves in the South escape to freedom prior to the Civil War.

in a country that established itself on Enlightenment principles and the idea that "all men are created equal … and endowed by their creator with certain inalienable rights … among [them] life, liberty, and the pursuit of happiness."

The United States tried to right the wrong of slavery by fighting a bloody Civil War, but it was not enough to root out racist ideas in the North or the South. Particularly in the South, segregation of blacks and whites became institutionalized over a period of approximately one hundred years between the Civil War and the civil rights movement of the 1950s and 1960s, which culminated in legal equality for African Americans and other minority groups across the United States. In the last sixty years, the country has made great attempts to change racial attitudes and become more socially just. Nonetheless, we have far to go.

There is still pervasive racism in our society that people of color must deal with on a regular basis. It is everyone's responsibility to look racism straight in the eye and take measures to create a just world and "a more perfect union." As Martin Luther King Jr. said, "Injustice anywhere is a threat to justice everywhere." There is no room for racism in America, and people of all colors need to show it the door.

CHAPTER ONE

A BRIEF HISTORY OF RACISM

Racism is the belief that people belong to different races and that, as a result, they have different capacities, temperaments, and limitations. Racism holds that one's own race is superior to all others. Racial discrimination is the differential treatment of people according to their perceived racial differences and implies favoring people of one's own race over all others.

The idea that human beings belong to different races has no basis in science; in fact, race is a social and political construct. The assignment of race is based on physical characteristics—primarily skin color, but also eye color, bone structure, and the color and texture of one's hair, as well as geographical origin. Some historians say that racism is fairly new in the world, created over the four centuries in which Europeans established racist regimes in Africa, Asia, and the Americas. However, earlier forms of xenophobia (fear or hatred of foreigners) were not so different from racism. For example, both the ancient Greeks and Chinese referred to outsiders as barbarians. While this term did not reference a specified race, it was a derogatory name for people who were "other" and considered to be inferior to the in-group. Islamic scholars expressed racist

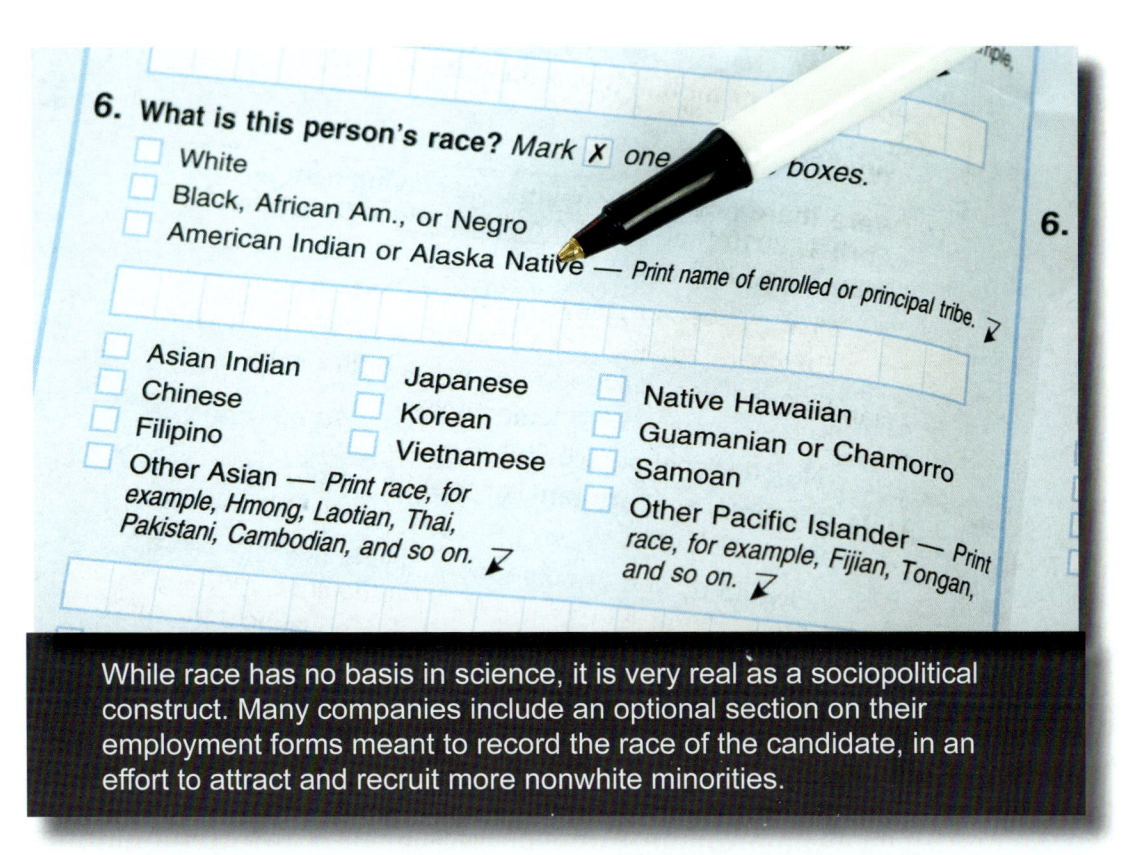

While race has no basis in science, it is very real as a sociopolitical construct. Many companies include an optional section on their employment forms meant to record the race of the candidate, in an effort to attract and recruit more nonwhite minorities.

views against sub-Saharan Africans in some of their medieval writings, and Jews were persecuted in Europe for two millennia because of their "otherness."

COLORISM: AN INTERNATIONAL PROBLEM

"Colorism" is a term coined by the American writer Alice Walker to refer to people's preference for the light-skinned over the dark-skinned, especially within one's own race or ethnic group. African Americans have felt the effects of colorism, both in their own communities as well as in society at large. But colorism is not new.

Alice Walker, a noted African American novelist, poet, essayist, and activist, has advocated for the rights of women and people of color both in the United States and globally.

India has a long history of skin-color prejudice that predates nineteenth-century British imperialism (and racism) on the subcontinent. Since its earliest history, Indian society was ordered by a rigid caste system, in which people were sorted according to occupation and religious status, and in which there was very little social mobility. The word for "caste" itself, *varna*, means "color." Moreover, those in the lower castes often have darker skin. The caste system in India has been outlawed but remains active in social life. In India, Japan, and other Asian countries, dark skin historically has been associated with those who labored outside. Thus, dark skin has carried the social stigma of poverty.

Colorism and discrimination based on skin color are problematic throughout the world. One indicator of colorism can be seen in the sale of skin whiteners, a multibillion dollar industry globally. According to a 2007 Nielson survey, 46 percent of Chinese, 47 percent of people in Hong Kong, 46 percent of Taiwanese, 29 percent of Koreans, and 24 percent of Japanese reported using skin lighteners in the previous year. By one estimate, 60 to 65 percent of Indian women use skin lightening products daily.

THE HGP DEBUNKS SCIENTIFIC BASIS FOR THE CONCEPT OF RACE

The Human Genome Project (HGP), completed in 2003, scientifically mapped the entirety of human hereditary material—three million base pairs of DNA that make up some nineteen to twenty thousand genes. The work of interpreting this data is still new and has opened the door to unprecedented advances in medicine and biotechnology. But equally important is that human gene mapping has proved there is no scientific basis for classifying people according to "subspecies," or races. Moreover, when people's DNA is compared, the genes differ by only about 0.1 percent. According to the Human Genome Project Information Archive:

> DNA studies do not indicate that separate classifiable subspecies (races) exist within modern humans. While different genes for physical traits such as skin and hair color can be identified between individuals, no consistent patterns of genes across the human genome exist to distinguish one race from another. There also is no genetic basis for divisions of human ethnicity. People who have lived in the same geographic region for many generations may have some alleles in common, but no allele will be found in all members of one population and in no members of any other.

(continued on the next page)

(continued from the previous page)

> *An allele is one or more alternative forms of a gene created by a mutation and found at the same place on a chromosome in everyone belonging to the same species. Human beings are among the least diverse of species, with only one in every 1,200 to 1,500 DNA bases (DNA bits) differing from one person to the next. On the level of DNA, we are 99.5 percent the same.*

SLAVERY AND RACISM

Slavery, or the making of chattel (items of property) of one group of people by another, is a universal phenomenon with a long history that unfortunately has not seen its end. Historically, enslaved people were made to work or used for sexual gratification and subject to terrible abuse. In many ancient and medieval societies, such as in Africa, the Middle East, Greece, and Rome, there could sometimes be a path to buying one's way out of slavery or rising in the social hierarchy. In some civilizations, the descendants of slaves mixed naturally into the general population after several generations. Although slaves were taken for granted in these societies, they were not generally thought to be inherently inferior to their captors, nor were they thought to be members of a subspecies of humans.

The first African slaves were brought to Jamestown, Virginia, in 1619 to help grow and harvest tobacco crops. By the eighteenth century, racism and slavery had formed a new, unholy alliance in the Americas—particularly in the United States. Thomas Jefferson, the author of the Declaration of Independence, wrote in his book *Notes on the State of Virginia* that "blacks, whether originally a distinct race, or made distinct by time and circumstances, are inferior to the whites in endowments both of body and mind." According to some historians, this view was necessary to justify policies (i.e., slavery) clearly contradictory to the idea that "all men are created equal." In this way, men of the Enlightenment—who professed a belief in human rights and the dignity of man—found it necessary to dehumanize the populations

The US government removed American Indian tribes from their homelands in the nineteenth century and forced them onto reservations. The government made and broke hundreds of treaties with native peoples.

they were exploiting for material gain. If the people they were exploiting were a subspecies, then the principles embodied in the Declaration of Independence and later the US Constitution simply did not apply to them.

European Americans applied a similar racist logic to American Indians, but for a different purpose. The Indians were deemed "uncivilizable" and pushed off their lands following the philosophy of "manifest destiny," a belief that European Americans had the right to expand "their" new nation from coast to coast.

As the country grew, so did its need for cheap labor. Particularly in the South, the practice of indentured servitude was phased out, while the plantation economy grew to demand a steady supply of free labor—in the form of black slaves. As time went on, laws were enacted to make slavery a permanent condition, passed on to one's children. By the 1840s, pseudo-scientific ideas about innate differences among races (white, black, and American Indian) gained traction. Black people were said to be inferior—and therefore, it was natural that they should be slaves.

In the notorious Dred Scott case of 1857, the Supreme Court ruled that people of African ancestry, whether enslaved or free, could never become citizens of the United States, because they "had no rights which the white man was bound to respect." With this ruling, the highest court in the nation had institutionalized racism in America, and it would take a bloody civil war to cut a new path toward a real American republic.

CHAPTER TWO

THE STRUGGLE FOR CIVIL RIGHTS AND RACIAL EQUALITY IN THE UNITED STATES

According to the US Census of 1860, there were 3,950,528 slaves living in America, some 13 percent of the population, and 476,748 "free colored persons." The American Civil War (1861–1865), a bloody conflict fought over Southern secession from the United States and the spread of slavery, ended in the Confederacy's defeat and return of the Southern states to the Union and the abolishment of slavery.

THE AFTERMATH OF THE CIVIL WAR

In the next several years, three amendments were added to the Constitution. The Thirteenth Amendment abolished "involuntary servitude," except in instances of punishment for a crime (1865). The Fourteenth Amendment defined citizens as people born in or naturalized in the United States, which made black children born in the United States citizens, while those born in Africa were eligible for citizenship (1868). The Fifteenth Amendment gave African American men the right to vote (1870). The Civil Rights Act of 1866 said that all citizens were entitled to equal protection under the law.

In reaction to these new requirements from the federal government, the Southern states in the former Confederacy enacted a series of laws known as "the Black codes," which aimed at keeping African Americans in a state of servitude. Vagrancy laws allowed police officers to arrest black people who were unemployed or without a permanent residence and bind them to a term of labor if they could not pay a fine.

The federal government established the Freedmen's Bureau in 1865 to help former slaves and poor whites in the South recover from the war. The Reconstruction Acts of 1867 worked to institute civil and political rights of African Americans. Despite these reforms, African Americans still had no land and often had to return as low-wage workers to the same plantations they had escaped. Soon white supremacist organizations like the Ku Klux Klan began to commit acts of terror against African Americans. By 1876, Reconstruction came to an end when the federal government withdrew and turned the South over to its old masters. By the turn of the century, black voters were largely unable to vote, and a rigid system of segregation had been reinstituted. African Americans were kept in line by threats of racist violence if they challenged the status quo.

PLESSY V. FERGUSON *RUBBER STAMPS SEGREGATION*

The Supreme Court decision that ushered in the Jim Crow era of widespread segregation was *Plessy v. Ferguson*, in which Homer Plessy tested the constitutionality of a Louisiana law passed in 1890. This law required railways to provide separate cars

THE STRUGGLE FOR CIVIL RIGHTS AND RACIAL EQUALITY IN THE UNITED STATES

Plessy v. Ferguson, a notorious Supreme Court case decided in 1896, ruled that so-called separate but equal accommodations of the races did not violate the Constitution, perpetuating widespread segregation in schools, such as this one.

for black and white passengers, each with the same accommodations. Homer Plessy was arrested for sitting in the whites-only car; his lawyer argued that the law violated the equal protection clause of the Fourteenth Amendment.

The court ruled that the Fourteenth Amendment was not meant to "enforce social as distinguished from political equality or a commingling of the two races upon terms unsatisfactory to either." Thus, the Supreme Court upheld the "separate but equal" justification for legal segregation. Jim Crow laws were quickly passed in the

South and the West. These laws set up dual systems of schooling and widespread segregation of the races and excluded nonwhites from mainstream public life.

BROWN V. BOARD OF EDUCATION

In 1954, the Supreme Court once again made a ruling that changed the course of civil rights history. *Brown v. Board of Education* was a combination of four class action suits brought by the National Association for the Advancement of Colored People (NAACP) on behalf of African American students who had been turned away from all-white schools. The court ruled unanimously that segregated educational facilities were "inherently unequal." Chief Justice Earl Warren ordered district courts and local school authorities to integrate public schools "with all deliberate speed." The South responded to the ruling with rage, and in one particularly high-profile case, the National Guard had to be called in to protect a handful of black students who integrated the all-white Little Rock Central High School in Arkansas in 1957.

Despite the work in the 1960s and 1970s to desegregate schools, integration in elementary and secondary education has still not been achieved. *De facto* segregation in all parts of the country (by reason of fact, not by law) remains a problem. For example, blacks and other minority populations who live in the inner cities of large metropolitan areas tend to send their children to schools that are filled mostly by minority children, while whites, who have moved to the suburbs, send their children to mostly white schools.

THE STRUGGLE FOR CIVIL RIGHTS AND RACIAL EQUALITY IN THE UNITED STATES

BLACK LIVES MATTER MOVEMENT

The civil rights movement may have wound down by the end of the 1960s, but civil rights activists have continued an unrelenting fight for racial equality in education, housing, the workplace, and all other areas of public life. While the United States has made some strides toward racial equality, the country has much further to go.

Black Lives Matter is a national movement for "the validity of black life." In February 2017, Nick Cannon joined leader Hawk Newsome and others from the movement to deliver a speech on activism to the South Bronx Community Charter School.

(continued on the next page)

(continued from the previous page)

> *The Black Lives Matter movement was begun by three female activists in 2012, after Trayvon Martin was killed by George Zimmerman, a member of a neighborhood watch group in Florida, who claimed he was defending himself against the unarmed black teenager. Zimmerman was acquitted under Florida's "Stand Your Ground" law. The Black Lives Matter movement seeks to resist dehumanization of black people and responds to anti-black racism. The movement has conducted protests in many parts of the country and has been especially visible in protesting instances of unnecessary police violence against unarmed people of color.*

THE CIVIL RIGHTS MOVEMENT

In 1955, Rosa Parks, a seamstress and civil rights activist who worked for the Montgomery, Alabama, chapter of the NAACP, refused to give up her seat to a white passenger on a public bus and was arrested as a result. The head of the local NAACP chapter, Edgar Nixon, seized the moment to call a bus boycott that launched the American civil rights movement. Dr. Martin Luther King Jr., a young minister at a local Baptist church in Montgomery, emerged as a community activist and boycott organizer.

In 1957, King and three other civil rights activists founded the Southern Christian Leadership Conference (SCLC) to coordinate actions that would challenge segregation and racial discrimination. The SCLC

Freedom Riders such as the ones pictured here risked their lives to ride through the South in integrated groups, challenging the enforcement (in violation of federal law) of segregated rest rooms and lunch counters in bus stations.

organized voter registration drives and was instrumental in organizing the 1963 March on Washington, during which Dr. King gave his famous "I Have a Dream" speech. King continued to lead civil rights protests and was planning a poor people's march on Washington right before his assassination in 1968.

The Student Nonviolent Coordinating Committee (SNCC), founded in 1960, used nonviolent protests to call attention to segregation. SNCC participated in Freedom Rides, begun in 1961, in which integrated teams of volunteers rode buses through the South and deliberately violated the segregation laws on the buses and in way stations. These laws had been ruled unconstitutional but were still being enforced. The Freedom Riders, mostly young people from across the United States, protested at great personal risk, and many of them were viciously beaten.

The nonviolent protests in the South received extensive press coverage. People across the United States watched activists, including children, beaten and hosed by the police on the nightly news, which helped arouse the nation's conscience. Racial equality seemed to be an idea whose time had come. The Civil Rights Act of 1964 and the Voting Rights Act of 1965 strengthened legal protections for African Americans. Nonetheless, protests continued across the nation, turning violent in major cities, from 1966 through 1968.

CHAPTER THREE

LEGAL PROTECTIONS AGAINST RACIAL DISCRIMINATION

As a result of the civil rights movement, Congress passed important legislation to guarantee the rights of people of all ethnicities. While the Constitution already guaranteed these rights, the new laws reinforced protections for people who had historically been discriminated against and made it easier to seek legal remedies if these laws were violated. Most of the problems you may encounter as a student will not end up in court, but it is important to know the extent of these legal protections, alongside their historical context.

VOTING RIGHTS

Section 2 of the Voting Rights Act of 1965 included a nationwide ban on literacy tests as a method of denying people the right to vote. Under Section 4 of the act, areas of the country with a history of suppressing voting rights were called out, and Section 5 prohibited those targeted areas from changing their voting rules until they were cleared with the attorney general or the US District Court of Washington, DC. This clearance requirement ensured that new voting rules would not have a discriminatory purpose or effect.

Targeted areas that needed to be monitored for voter suppression were first determined by whether or not jurisdictions had used a test or device to restrict voting, and in circumstances where fewer than half of the people of voting age were registered to vote in that area. Over time, the law was tweaked to ensure the voting rights of language minority groups. Jurisdictions were added or allowed to "bail out" if it was determined that they had met the standards of the law. The Supreme Court issued additional decisions in the early years of the Voting Rights Act to affirm the constitutionality of Section 5 and the kinds of voting practices that might need review before a state or local voting rule was changed. The use of poll taxes in national elections had been prohibited by the Twenty-Fourth Amendment to the Constitution, passed in 1964.

In 2013, the Supreme Court ruled in *Shelby County v. Holder* that Section 4 (b) of the Voting Rights Act was unconstitutional. This is the section that determines which jurisdictions need preclearance from the Attorney General or the District Court before changing their voting rules. The new Supreme Court ruled 5-4 that Section 4 (b) was unconstitutional because the data that determined which jurisdictions needed to be monitored was out of date. While the Court upheld Section 5, this section is useless without Section 4 (b), and new rules have not been made by Congress thus far to determine which jurisdictions need oversight. As a result, seventeen states put new voter restrictions in place for the 2016 presidential election. Some examples of what the new rules require include: photo IDs for voting; elimination of same-day or out-of-precinct voting; shorter time periods for voter registration before elections;

elimination of preregistration of sixteen- and seventeen-year-olds; and elimination of early voting.

CIVIL RIGHTS

President John Kennedy first introduced a civil rights bill into Congress in 1963. After Kennedy's assassination, President Lyndon Johnson took an aggressive role in getting the bill through Congress, marshaling supporters and sidelining opponents. A filibuster in the Senate held up the bill for an additional fifty-seven days, after which it was signed into law.

THE CIVIL RIGHTS ACT OF 1964

The Civil Rights Act of 1964 outlawed discrimination based on race, color, religion, sex, and national origin. A voting rights portion of the act required voting rules and procedures to be applied equally to all races. Discrimination was prohibited in all public accommodations (such as hotels, motels, and restaurants) engaged in interstate commerce and in public facilities of state and municipal governments. Any government agency that received federal funds was also subject to the provisions of the act.

Title IV encouraged school desegregation and gave the US attorney general latitude to file suits to enforce the act. Title VII prohibited discrimination in employment for any employer with fifteen or more employees and created the Equal Employment Opportunity Commission (EEOC).

The act also expanded the powers of the Civil Rights Commission, requiring that voter registration and voting

CONFRONTING RACISM

The historic 1963 March on Washington, where Dr. Martin Luther King Jr. delivered his famous "I Have a Dream" speech, brought about a quarter of a million people to the capital to demand jobs and equal rights.

statistics be compiled in geographic areas specified by the commission. Title IX made it easier to move civil rights cases from state to federal courts.

FAIR HOUSING ACT

Also called Title VII of the Civil Rights Act of 1968, the Fair Housing Act protected people from discrimination in buying, selling, or renting housing based on race, religion, or national origin and was later expanded to protect people based on gender, disability, or family status (people with children). The Fair Housing Act did not generally apply to buildings of less than five apartments when the owner occupied one of those apartments. Thus, the owner of such a building could refuse to rent to people in minority groups.

The same was true, for the most part, in renting or selling a private house. If a renter or seller went through a broker, however, the Fair Housing Act would still apply. Thus, real-estate agencies were not allowed to "steer" people toward or away from certain properties based on race or any other category.

EQUAL EMPLOYMENT OPPORTUNITY ACT OF 1972

Before the passage of this act, the EEOC had no effective enforcement authority, since it had to refer discrimination claims to the Department of Justice. This new act defined discrimination in employment and gave the EEOC the power to litigate (not just investigate) discrimination cases—that is, bring them to court.

CIVIL RIGHTS ACT OF 1991

This act was passed after a series of US Supreme Court decisions limited the rights of employees to sue their employers for discrimination. The act provided the right to a jury trial for discrimination claims and introduced the possible provision of damages based on emotional distress.

Residents of Camden, New Jersey, film a police officer while protesting police brutality during a visit from then-president Barack Obama in May 2015. When the 90 percent minority community of South Camden sued the state of New Jersey in 2001, they didn't know their decision would help lead to the passage of the Civil Rights Act of 2004.

CIVIL RIGHTS ACT OF 2004

Sometimes call the Fairness Act, this legislation was also passed in response to several US Supreme Court decisions that had ruled against people seeking remedies for civil rights violations in school and the workplace.

One part of the act confirmed that people could get legal relief from practices in federally funded programs that had resulted in discrimination. People could sue under Title VI of the Civil Rights Act of 1964, Title IX of the Education Amendments of 1972 (protecting girls and women), and the Age Discrimination and Employment Act of 1975.

Other parts of the act addressed other types of discrimination and mentioned additional laws under which people could seek legal relief.

ALTERNATIVE AVENUES FOR CHANGE

Not all of the problems you may encounter involving discrimination in the classroom or community can be fixed under the current framework of the law, but it is still important to call attention to these issues as you see them. In 2014, the Education Fund of the Texas Freedom Network, an activist group that monitors the far right, published its findings of an extensive scholarly review of forty-three history and geography textbooks created for the Texas market. They found extensive problems in the materials. History textbooks, for example, glossed over the effects of Jim Crow laws and implied that the separate schools for blacks and whites were somewhat comparable. One textbook referred to slavery in the context of immigration, as if African slaves came to America as immigrant workers.

As it turns out, the Texas school board had established a curriculum in 2010 with a distinct bias toward portraying the United States as a nation founded on Judeo-Christian principles and biblical law, with a focus on promoting American patriotism. With this agenda in hand, the school board had then commissioned textbook companies to produce these materials.

While they offered to print corrections, one hundred thousand of these textbooks had already been purchased by Texas, and another forty thousand were in schools nationwide. If you notice something strange

CONFRONTING RACISM

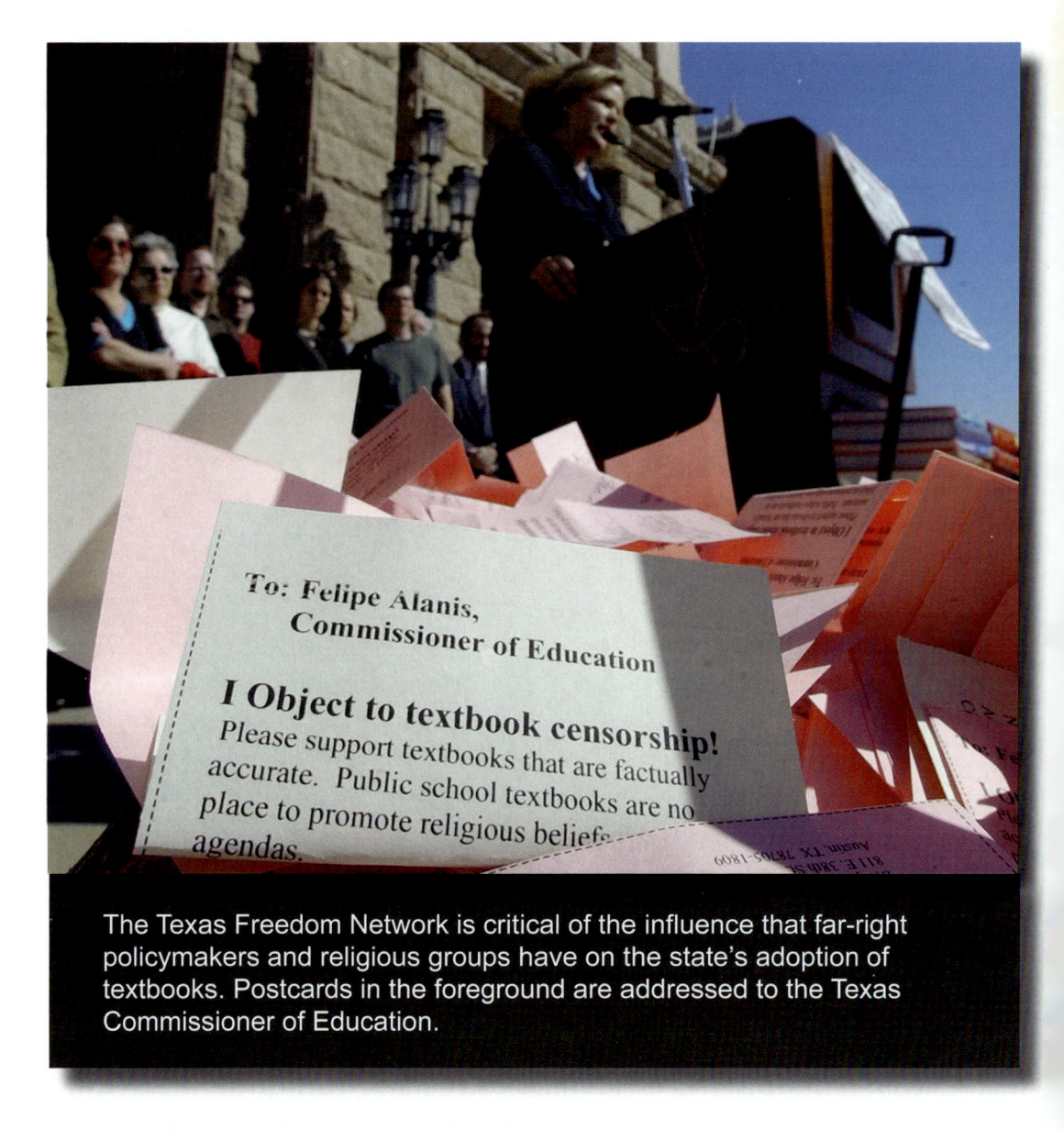

The Texas Freedom Network is critical of the influence that far-right policymakers and religious groups have on the state's adoption of textbooks. Postcards in the foreground are addressed to the Texas Commissioner of Education.

going on at your school or in the world around you, say something. Consider the potential of your own influence on your state's board of education, and the influence of your peers. By speaking up, you may find that an entire network of people are already on your side.

MYTHS AND FACTS

MYTH
Unlike the textbooks of the past, today's textbooks are free of cultural bias.

Fact
Political agendas often dictate what goes into textbooks, because writers and editors follow guidelines set by a state or a large school district. If a school board establishes a curriculum with a distinct bias, then the textbook companies commissioned to produce their materials will be more likely to produce biased materials as well.

MYTH
History books and textbooks provide an objective account of what happened in the past.

Fact
There is no such thing as an objective account of history, because any document that provides the basis for history or any remembered account is always a point of view. Anyone reading or listening to first-person accounts must interpret what they see, hear, or read through their own understanding and cultural lens. Any account of history is presented as a story, and it is not possible to write a story without creating an interpretation, which is inherently biased. The best that can be done is to include as many viewpoints as possible to correct for personal and cultural bias.

(continued on the next page)

A 2016 report from the Education Trust found that in more than half of 234 surveyed public colleges, gaps between black and white graduation rates either stayed the same or increased from 2003 to 2013.

the person to support his or her assertions with facts. When it comes to jokes, speak up and say that you find them offensive. Politely ask the offender not to repeat them.

It's natural for people to feel uncomfortable when confronted, so be prepared for a verbal attack or an accusation that you have no sense of humor or just misunderstood what was said. But if you are able to keep calm, you can point to the words you found offensive and explain why. The person who made the remark may not apologize or take it back, but he or she may think twice about repeating such remarks in the future.

When slurs and hateful remarks are made by one person to another with the intention of inflicting social or psychological damage, it is best to get help from a teacher, guidance counselor, principal, supervisor, or another person in authority. When enlisting the help of an authority figure, repeat the offensive remarks as precisely as you can remember them, without minimizing or embellishing. Tell the person in authority that you are aware that such speech constitutes unlawful harassment under the Civil Rights Act of 1964. This is true whether you are at school or in a workplace.

If you report such behavior, you have a right to know what will be done to put a stop to the harassment. This applies whether you are reporting harassment against yourself or someone else. Follow up, and get your parents involved in the process. Sometimes a person who is acting as a bully or creating a hostile environment will stop after being counseled. If he or she is having an argument with another person and the offensive behavior grew out of a disagreement, peer mediation may disarm opponents and teach them to get along with each other. However, if the hate speech continues, ask for swift disciplinary action. If the offensive behavior is not stopped, go to a higher authority—the school superintendent or the head of human resources, for example—to have the problem resolved.

CONFRONTING INSTANCES OF UNEQUAL TREATMENT

Suppose your friend Hannah turns to you for advice. She has been successfully working at a fast food restaurant for a year and has received two positive reviews and even a small raise. A managerial position opens on her shift and she applies. Hannah is turned down, and the promotion is given to another worker, Emily, who has been with the company only six months. Hannah, who is black, suspects that she has been passed over for promotion because of her race. When she asks her boss about his decision, he says that he thinks the other shift workers would be uncomfortable having Hannah as their boss. He doesn't give a reason for their discomfort. Besides, he says, Emily understands them better. Emily

The Equal Employment Act of 1972 defined discrimination in employment, and Executive Order 11246 of 1965 mandated that government contractors show they are taking "affirmative action" to recruit and hire members of underrepresented groups.

is the same age as Hannah, but she is white—like the rest of the shift workers. It would appear that Hannah's boss is just unwilling to put a black person in charge of a crew of white workers.

EXECUTIVE ORDER 11246 OF 1965 AND AFFIRMATIVE ACTION

Executive Order 11246 prohibits US government contractors, subcontractors, and federally assisted construction contractors from discriminating in employment or hiring practices based on race, color, religion, sex, or national origin. The law applies to all those contractors doing more than $10,000 worth of business with the government yearly. Service and supply contractors with more than fifty employees and contractors doing at least $50,000 worth of business yearly with the government must have affirmative action plans in place to increase the number of women and minorities in their workforce if they are underrepresented. They must also keep employment records of their recruitment, hiring, and actions to show they are complying with the law.

Contrary to popular belief, affirmative action does not establish "quotas" that must be filled by minorities or women. Rather, contractors must show that they have made a good faith effort to hire people in underrepresented categories.

With such a scenario, you should advise Hannah to take her complaint to human resources and tell them she has reason to believe she's been denied a promotion on the basis of her race. Hannah should cite the manager's unequal treatment of her, which is prohibited by the Civil Rights Acts of 1964, 1991, and 2004. Advise Hannah to document all conversations with both her boss and human resources, and encourage her to stand up for herself and demand that the company address her complaint. If they do not, she can file a complaint with the Equal Employment Opportunity Commission (EEOC).

BECOMING AN ACTIVIST

It is never too early to become an activist. Think about joining a student group that fights against discrimination or promotes racial equality or social justice. Some of the national groups that work for racial justice have youth memberships—for example, the NAACP (National Association for the Advancement of Colored People). These groups are particularly directed at students, while others sponsor programs for students. For example, RISE (The Ross Initiative in Sports for Equality) offers educational programs to student-athletes at the secondary and tertiary level. Their Leadership Program addresses matters of racism, prejudice, diversity, and inclusivity within the students' teams, schools, and communities. Additionally, the Congress for Racial Equality hosts a Civil Rights Boot Camp on Practical Training in Respect and Understanding. This one hundred hour program offers sensitivity training in diversity.

SPOTTING AND ADDRESSING OVERT RACIAL DISCRIMINATION | 39

The NAACP is an activist organization that encourages young people to work toward racial equality and fight against stereotyping. These student athletes took part in a campaign to promote positive statistics about young black men.

Another way to get involved is by calling and writing to your congressional representatives and senators about social justice issues. You can also start a club or group in your school for people interested in racial equality and in bridging the racial divide. Together you can work on the local level in your school and community to address discrimination and promote fairness and equity.

CHAPTER FIVE

SPOTTING AND ADDRESSING COVERT DISCRIMINATION IN THE CLASSROOM

Covert racial discrimination is a subtle form of bias in which people's prejudices are disguised or rationalized. Covert racial discrimination can sometimes be worse than overt discrimination because it creates an ongoing situation in which people belonging to a minority group are uncertain about their own perceptions. Moreover, when it goes unchecked, covert racism promotes biased perceptions of minority groups that are internalized by both majority and minority groups. Covert bias may not be intentional—that is, people may not be conscious of their own prejudices. Therefore, sometimes the solution to covert racial discrimination is simply to shine the light of awareness on unconscious biases.

UNCONSCIOUS BIAS IN THE CLASSROOM

A study conducted by the Yale University Child Center may provide some clues about the differential suspension rate of white and black children in preschool programs. Black children made up about 19 percent of preschool students in 2013 to 2014, but they also

SPOTTING AND ADDRESSING COVERT DISCRIMINATION IN THE CLASSROOM

accounted for about 47 percent of suspensions. To understand why this might be the case, a group of 130 preschool teachers were asked to watch video clips and look for signs of "challenging behavior." In fact, there were no instances of misbehavior in the clips, but researchers tracked teachers' eye movements and found they looked at boys more than girls and black children more than white children. They observed black boys 42 percent of the time and white boys 34 percent of the time, confirming where they expected to find the challenging behaviors. As part of the same study, teachers were read stories about students misbehaving.

A study conducted by the Yale University Child Center found that while preschool-aged boys were being observed 76 percent of the time, black girls commanded only 10 percent of their preschool teachers' attention. Teachers must be hypervigilant about unconscious racial bias.

White teachers conveyed more lenient attitudes toward such behavior from black students than from white children, while conversely black teachers held the black children to a higher standard.

A different study out of New York University asked teachers to read case studies about male students and disclose the likelihood that they would refer each student to either special education or gifted testing. When teachers read studies of boys with good academics and emotional sensitivity, they were more likely to choose white students for gifted testing than black or Latino students. In turn, when they read about boys with academic challenges, they also chose white students for special education testing over students of color. But when they read about boys with behavioral challenges, teachers were most likely to refer black and Latino boys for special education testing. This research would support the hypothesis that teachers fail to recognize high ability among students of color, and are more likely to perceive low academic performance from students of color as "normal," whereas they expect black boys to be more aggressive and problematic than white boys.

CONFRONTING TEACHER BIAS

Biased teacher behavior in a classroom can take many forms, resulting in harsher discipline, lower expectations, and fewer chances to interact for students of color. For example, a teacher may unconsciously call on white students more often than black students or may not positively reinforce black students as much as white students. Most teachers have good intentions and believe they are not biased. Some may even say they

SPOTTING AND ADDRESSING COVERT DISCRIMINATION IN THE CLASSROOM

Teachers need to maintain high expectations for students of all races and ethnicities. No one is "color blind," and educators have a special duty to monitor themselves for prejudice or bias in the classroom.

are "color blind." Teachers are human beings, and sometimes they simply favor some students—and they may not believe their preferences are motivated by race. They may work hard to be fair and fail.

If you feel that a teacher is racially biased, enlist the help of an adult advocate in confronting the problem—whether this advocate is a guidance counselor, parent, guardian, or even another teacher. In discussing your feelings and perceptions with a sympathetic adult, be as fair as possible. Note specific instances of what you perceive as biased behavior on the part of a teacher. Unfounded or vague accusations will not help in these situations. You might ask your adult advocate to arrange a three-way meeting. Most teachers will give you a chance to be heard and attempt to address your concerns if you approach them with respect.

However, the teacher will most likely be approaching the situation with a different viewpoint from your own. Be open minded when speaking to your teacher about perceived bias, and be prepared to consider whether your perceptions are entirely accurate. An honest, open conversation without finger pointing or name calling will be most productive for remedying problematic behavior or interactions. Furthermore, if you feel as if the materials that are being used in class are racially biased, do some research and bring alternative points of view to the attention of your teacher in the form of printed materials from reputable sources.

IS IT EVER OK TO USE THE N-WORD?

It is common for people of color and other minority students perceived as being part of an "in-group" of black students to call each other the n-word. We can identify the word quite often—even when it is censored—when we listen to the song lyrics of some current musical artists. Sometimes, the n-word is used as a weapon by a white person against a black person. This usually leads to a serious racial incident. Other times, a white person uses the n-word without known intent of malice, in a way he or she thinks is similar to how black people use it, but this almost always draws the ire of that person's black friends and acquaintances.

Is it ever OK for a person to address another person using the n-word—even when both people are black? According to one sociological view, this reclamation of the most dreadful racial slur by black people has taken the sting out of it. This point of view would uphold that black people use the n-word affectionately with one another—but in truth, this is often not the case. People of color can just as easily use the word as an insult, even when it's said in the context of a jest. A recent blog post from The Black Institute said in a reflection titled "Can We Ever Really Reclaim the 'N' Word?":

> After the word was created it was used for over [five] centuries in the United States of America to denigrate, belittle, and shame the very population of people on whose backs this country was forged. Yet somehow, in the last [fifty] years, this word which carries incalculable pain of ancestors past, has become a basic fixture in the Black vernacular.

The unnamed writer continues by asking the reader and his or herself, "How can we reclaim a word that can still cause us pain when it comes out of the wrong mouth?" and offering his or her response: "Until that time comes when the word ... has been neutralized and can no longer be used to diminish, demean, or otherwise torment Black people, reclaiming it seems simply impossible." We could all be patient—or, just make the conscious choice never to use it, even in jest.

OPENING CONVERSATIONS ABOUT RACE

Think about ways in which you can open conversations about race at school without putting people on the defensive. Does your school conduct special activities during Black History Month? Perhaps more can be done to involve all students, not only in celebrating African American heritage but also in thinking about how to improve race relations.

Watching films can be an inclusive and accessible way of highlighting the contributions marginalized groups have made to society. *Hidden Figures* (2016) exposes a variety of roles that black female mathematicians played in NASA's early space programs.

Students continue to show patterns of self-segregation during social activities, even in well-integrated schools. It is not uncommon to see students segregated in the cafeteria by table. Why is this the case? It may be possible to begin a schoolwide dialogue about this pervasive phenomenon. Think about ways in which you and your peers can cross the racial divide.

Students who attend schools that are primarily white or primarily black often have little opportunity to engage in interracial interactions. Perhaps you can talk to your principal or guidance counselor about arranging a social or educational event in which two schools with ethnically or racially different populations can do something together, providing everyone with an opportunity to meet people outside of their own group. Sometimes racism is triggered by fear of the unknown "other," and it is only with exposure that such fears can be eliminated.

CHAPTER SIX

STAYING HEALTHY IN A WORLD THAT IS NOT POSTRACIAL

President Barack Obama noted in his farewell address of 2016, "After my election, there was talk of a post-racial America. Such a vision, however well intended, was never realistic. Race remains a potent and often divisive force in our society." This is as true today as it was when the first African American president was elected in 2008. Despite the progress we have made, racism is still a serious problem in the United States, and people of color still experience inequality in education, opportunity, and in the justice system. But the United States is still a young country, and the civil rights movement is not even one hundred years old.

While all Americans must cope with this country's racial history, it bears down most heavily on people of color. This is especially true for African Americans, but the weight of history also falls on Hispanic Americans, Asian Americans, and many immigrants. For people of color, racial discrimination is personal. But from another perspective, it isn't *personal* at all. A racist who is acting out does not see a person—he or she sees only his or her own projection of hatred or fear. Therefore, in confronting racism, it is important to remember to step

STAYING HEALTHY IN A WORLD THAT IS NOT POSTRACIAL | 49

At the 2015 White House Correspondents' Dinner, President Barack Obama invited actor Keegan-Michael Key onstage to reprise his role as Luther, Obama's anger translator, from the TV show *Key and Peele*. Many feel that Obama would have been criticized if he had expressed himself fully, as a black man in the position of US president.

back and remind yourself that it is not about you but about someone else's ignorance. Nonetheless, racism cannot be ignored. Blatant forms of racism are easier to recognize, confront, and possibly remedy. Subtle forms of racism present a greater challenge.

TYPES OF MICROAGGRESSIONS

Microaggressions are statements or action of indirect, sometimes unintentional, discrimination. According to Tori DeAngelis, the term "racial microaggressions" was first used by psychiatrist Chester M. Pierce in the 1970s, but psychologist Derald Wing Sue has further classified such behavior in three categories of microassaults, microinsults, and microinvalidations:

Microassaults are intentional actions meant to belittle a person of color, such as wearing racist insignia or treating a person of color with obvious disrespect. Microassaults are in the category of overt racism.

Microinsults are verbal or nonverbal communications that are rude or insensitive and demean a person's racial identity. Microinsults are often covert. For example, a white college freshman might ask a black college freshman at an ivy-league school how he or she scored on the SAT test, implying that the admission was based on affirmative action.

Microinvalidations are communications that subtly exclude or negate the thoughts, feelings, or experiences of a person of color. These actions are often covert and sometimes subconscious. For example, an Asian American may be asked what country he or she is from. Consistently being taken for a foreigner is a common experience for Asian Americans. The most blatant example of the "aliening" of Asian Americans was the incarceration of Japanese Americans during World War II.

COPING WITH MICROAGGRESSIONS

One way to address micoassaults and microinsults is to call people's attention to them calmly. Once again, it will be important to specifically point out which part of the person's speech is offensive and why it is offensive. If the microassault or insult involves stereotyping, this may be an opportunity to dispel a racial prejudice. Ask the person about whether his or her belief has any basis in fact. This will be an effective strategy when people aren't aware of their own biases and do not perceive themselves as prejudiced. Such people believe they are not racists and *do not want to be racists*, but they may need help recognizing their unconscious and deeply held biases.

Some people have no capacity or desire for self-reflection, and if you confront them about a microaggression, they may accuse you of being overly sensitive or of misrepresenting their words or intentions. When people enter into denial, it is useless to argue with them. If their words do not have any direct or immediate impact on your life or well-being, it may be best to disengage from them or ignore them. Everyone in life has to pick their battles, and sometimes it just makes more sense to walk away from ignorance.

We all need a support network of friends, family, and cheerleaders. In coping with racism, turn to the people

> Having an emotionally painful, honest conversation about race can be one of the most productive ways to make unconscious biases conscious. However, if the person you are confronting appears upset or angry, it is OK to remove yourself from the situation and try a different approach at a later date.

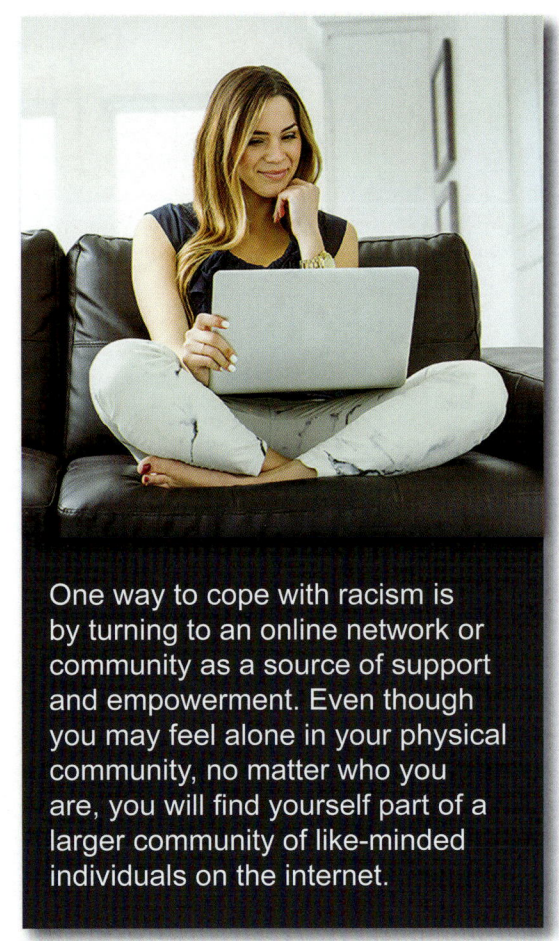

One way to cope with racism is by turning to an online network or community as a source of support and empowerment. Even though you may feel alone in your physical community, no matter who you are, you will find yourself part of a larger community of like-minded individuals on the internet.

who love and care about you to express your anger or hurt and to get validation of your worthiness. Networking with people of color who are facing similar challenges can also provide validation. Taking a leadership role in your school, workplace, or community will help you feel empowered, as will joining a group that works for racial equality or social justice.

Finally, it is important to cultivate relationships with people outside your racial group. Many people of all ethnicities are working toward social justice. Martin Luther King Jr. said, "Injustice anywhere is a threat to justice everywhere. We are caught in an inescapable network of mutuality, tied in a single garment of destiny. Whatever affects one directly, affects all indirectly." When we diminish another person, we also diminish ourselves, and that is why racism hurts everybody. Expect the best from people, and don't assume without evidence that they are biased. It is important to look inward to determine and deal with one's own prejudices before confronting racial discrimination in the community. Remember that when you have high expectations of people, they are more likely to rise to your standards.

10 GREAT QUESTIONS
TO ASK YOURSELF

1. Do I feel fear when I see or pass a stranger who does not belong to my race or ethnic group?

2. Do I feel uncomfortable when I see a mixed-race couple? If so, why do I feel uncomfortable?

3. Am I afraid that people of other races or ethnicities will think I am a racist?

4. Do I avoid people of other races or ethnicities because I am not sure how to act with them?

5. Do I tend to remember negative information about other racial groups and forget positive information that I may have read or heard?

6. Do I hold stereotypical beliefs about race? If so, do I have any clear factual evidence to support my beliefs?

7. Do I tell racist or ethnic jokes or laugh when others tell such jokes?

8. Do I think that all white people are racists? Do I think that all black people hate white people?

9. Do I think people of color are not as smart as white people?

10. Do I think it's impossible to bridge the racial divide?

GLOSSARY

barbarian A derogatory term for someone outside of one's racial or ethnic group that indicates the outsider is considered to be inferior.

bias A judgment based on a faulty assumption, usually with no basis in fact. A bias can be either in favor of or against the person or thing in question.

civil rights The rights of individuals to fair and equal treatment under the law. In the United States, civil rights are outlined in the first ten amendments to the Constitution.

colorism A bias in favor of light skin over dark skin that occurs either within the same ethnic group or among ethnic groups.

constitutionality Refers to the legal test of whether a law, practice, or court verdict is allowable or correct according to the United States Constitution.

de facto segregation Refers to the separation of races or ethnic groups that occurs by virtue of circumstances. Sometimes those circumstances are deliberately created to promote segregation.

denial A psychological defense mechanism, often subconscious, in which a person refuses to confront or admit to a personal problem or something in reality.

DNA Deoxyribonucleic acid, a self-replicating material that is the main component of chromosomes in any living being; the carrier of genetic information.

harassment From a legal perspective, the systematic and continued actions, up to and inclusive of threats, demands, and hate speech, of one person toward another. Harassment that is based in racism often takes the form of bullying.

The Human Genome Project An international science research project completed in 2003 that determined the sequence of all the base pairs that make up human DNA; this debunked the idea of separate races, since there is little diversity from person to person or group to group on the level of DNA.

Jim Crow Refers to a caricature of African Americans common in so-called minstrel shows that took place in the nineteenth and twentieth centuries; segregation laws in the South came to be called Jim Crow laws.

microaggression A statement or action of indirect, sometimes unintentional, discrimination that expresses prejudice toward a member of a marginalized group, such as a racial minority.

prejudice A preconceived notion about an individual not based in fact or experience.

racial discrimination The practice of treating someone differently—often unfairly or cruelly—on the basis of their perceived race or ethnicity. Racial discrimination implies a dislike, aversion, or hatred for people in a given racial or ethnic group.

racial segregation The deliberate separation of people according to perceived race or ethnicity.

racism The practice of discrimination against someone perceived as belonging to a different race beginning with the assumption that one's own race is superior to another race or races.

species A biological classification of related organisms capable of interbreeding and exchanging genes and having the same general characteristics.

stereotyping The practice of assigning characteristics to an individual according to prejudices or biases held about the group to which that person belongs.

xenophobia Fear or hatred of strangers, foreigners, or people not in the "in-group."

FOR MORE INFORMATION

American Civil Liberties Union
125 Broad Street, 18th Floor
New York, NY 10004
(212) 549-2500
Website: https://www.aclu.org
Facebook: @aclu.nationwide
Twitter: @aclu
YouTube: @acluvideos

The ACLU is almost one hundred years old. Its mission is to defend and preserve individual rights and the liberties guaranteed by the Constitution. The ACLU has local affiliates as well as an information-rich website. The organization solicits donations that help it carry on its work, wherein a donation grants that person membership to the ACLU.

Brown v. Board of Education National Historic Site
515 SE Monroe Street
Topeka, KS 66612-1143
(785) 354-4273
Website: https://www.nps.gov/brvb/index.htm
Facebook: @nationalparkservice
Twitter: @NatlParkService
Instagram: @nationalparkservice
YouTube: @NationalParkService

This is the national historic site of Monroe Elementary School and its grounds, one of the four segregated elementary schools for African American children in Topeka at the time of the *Brown* decision in 1954. The national historic site commemorates *Brown v. Board of Education*.

FOR MORE INFORMATION | 57

Canadian Human Rights Commission
344 Slater Street, 8th Floor
Ottawa, ON K1A 1E1
Canada
(888) 214-1090
Website: https://www.chrc-ccdp.ca/eng
Facebook: @CanadianHumanRightsCommission
Twitter: @CdnHumanRights
The Canadian Human Rights Commission helps Canadians fight discrimination in their daily lives. The commission also receives and resolves discrimination complaints.

Canadian Human Rights International Organization (CHRIO)
1725 Finch Avenue
West Toronto, ON M3N 1M6
Canada
(416) 635-7805 / (416) 907-6631
Website: http://www.chrio.ca
Twitter: @CHRIOCANADA
Instagram: @chriocanada
This organization is made up of professionals practicing law, social work, sociology, psychology, and criminology. It also includes human rights advocates. CHRIO monitors human rights abuses and works to eliminate them.

Equal Employment Opportunity Commission
131 M Street NE
Washington, DC 20507
(202) 663-4900
Website: https://www.eeoc.gov
Facebook: @USEEOC

Twitter: @USEEOC
YouTube: @TheEEOC
The EEOC enforces federal laws that make it illegal to discriminate against job applicants or employees because of race, color, religion, sex (including pregnancy, gender identity, and sexual orientation), national origin, age (forty or older), disability, or genetic information. The EEOC has fifty-three affiliates.

Southern Poverty Law Center (SPLC)
400 Washington Avenue
Montgomery, AL 36104
(334) 956-8200 / (888) 414-7752
Website: https://www.splcenter.org
Facebook: @SPLCenter
Twitter: @splcenter
The Southern Poverty Law Center's mission is to fight racism and to seek justice for the most vulnerable members of society. The SPLC uses litigation (lawsuits), education, and other forms of advocacy to move the country toward equality. SPLC is well known for its Teaching Tolerance education materials.

WEBSITES

Because of the changing nature of internet links, Rosen Publishing has developed an online list of websites related to the subject of this book. This site is updated regularly. Please use this link to access this list:

http://www.rosenlinks.com/SPKUP/Racism

FOR FURTHER READING

Alexander, Michelle. *The New Jim Crow: Mass Incarceration in the Age of Colorblindness*. New York, NY: The New Press, 2010.

Coates, Ta-Nehisi. *Between the World and Me*. New York, NY: Spiegel & Grau, 2015.

Fremon, David K. *The Jim Crow Laws and Racism in United States History* (In United States History). Berkeley Heights, NJ: Enslow Publishers, 2015.

Grinipol, Corinne. *Racial Profiling and Discrimination: Your Legal Rights* (Know Your Rights). New York, NY: Rosen Publishing, 2016.

Hanson-Harding, Alexandra. *I've Been Racially Profiled. Now What?* (Teen Life 411). New York, NY: Rosen Publishing, 2015.

Henneberg, Susan, ed. *Race in America* (Opposing Viewpoints Series). New York, NY: Greenhaven Publishing, 2017.

Kendi, Ibram X. *Stamped from the Beginning: The Definitive History of Racist Ideas in America*. New York, NY: Nation Books, 2017.

Purdum, Todd S. *An Idea Whose Time Has Come. Two Presidents, Two Parties, and the Battle for the Civil Rights Act of 1964*. New York, NY: Henry Holt and Company, 2014.

Rajczak, Kristen. *The Civil Right Movement in Texas* (Spotlight on Texas). New York, NY: PowerKids Press, 2014.

Wallis, Jim. *America's Original Sin: Racism, White Privilege, and the Bridge to a New America*. Grand Rapids, MI: Brazos Press, 2016.

BIBLIOGRAPHY

The Black Institute. "Can We Ever Really Reclaim the 'N' Word?" *Black Ops*, August 3, 2011. http://www.theblackinstitute.org/can_we_ever_really_reclaim_the_n_word.

Brown, Emma. "Yale Study Suggests Racial Bias Among Preschool Teachers." *Washington Post*, September 27, 2016. https://www.washingtonpost.com/news/education/wp/2016/09/27/yale-study-suggests-racial-bias-among-preschool-teachers.

Constitutional Rights Foundation. "The Civil Rights Act of 1964." 2017. http://www.crf-usa.org/black-history-month/the-civil-rights-act-of-1964.

DeAngelis, Tori. "Unmasking Racial Microaggressions." American Psychological Association. February 2009. http://www.apa.org/monitor/2009/02/microaggression.aspx.

Hathaway, Bill. "Implicit Bias May Help Explain High Preschool Expulsion Rates for Black Children." *Yale News*, September 27, 2016. http://news.yale.edu/2016/09/27/implicit-bias-may-help-explain-high-preschool-expulsion-rates-black-children.

Human Genome Project Information Archive, 1990–2003. "Minorities, Race, and Genomics." US Department of Energy Office of Science, Office of Biological and Environmental Research. August 6, 2013. http://web.ornl.gov/sci/techresources/Human_Genome/elsi/minorities.shtml.

Jones, Trina. "Significance of Skin Color in Asian and Asian-American Communities: Initial Reflections." *UC Irvine Law Review*, December 2013. http://www.law.uci.edu/lawreview/vol3/no4/Jones.pdf.

King, Martin Luther, Jr. "Letter from a Birmingham Jail."

African Studies Center, University of Pennsylvania. April 16, 1963. http://www.africa.upenn.edu/Articles_Gen/Letter_Birmingham.html.

Nesoff, Jeremy. "The Myth of a Post-Racial Society After the Obama Presidency." *Facing Today, A Facing History Blog*, February 8, 2017. http://facingtoday.facinghistory.org/the-myth-of-a-post-racial-society-after-the-obama-presidency.

New York University. "Race Influences Teachers' Referrals to Special and Gifted Education, Finds Steinhardt Study." News Release, October 18, 2016. https://www.nyu.edu/about/news-publications/news/2016/october/race-influences-teachers-referrals-to-special-and-gifted-educati.html.

Perry, Mark. "Perceptions of Race in the Arab World." *Perceptions of Blackness and Whiteness in the Middle East*. http://inhouse.lau.edu.lb/bima/papers/Perry.pdf.

Richie, Nigel. *The Civil Rights Movement, Lives in Crisis*. New York, NY: Barron's Educational Series, 2003.

Texas Freedom Network Education Fund. *Writing to the Standards: Reviews of Proposed Social Studies Textbooks for Texas Public Schools*. Executive Summary, September 2014. http://tfn.org/cms/assets/uploads/2015/11/FINAL_executivesummary.pdf.

Timmons, Heather. "Telling India's Modern Women They Have Power, Even Over Their Skin Tone." *New York Times*, May 30, 2007. http://www.nytimes.com/2007/05/30/business/media/30adco.html?r=1&ref=business&oref=slogin.

Wong, Alia. "History Class and the Fictions About Race in America." *Atlantic*, October 21, 2015. https://www.theatlantic.com/education/archive/2015/10/the-history-class-dilemma/411601.

INDEX

B

bias
  recognizing, 51, 52
  teacher, 41, 42–43, 44
  unconscious, 40–41, 51
Black Lives Matter, 19, 20
Brown v. Board of Education, 18

C

Civil Rights Act of 1964, 22,
    25–26, 28, 35
Civil Rights Commission, 25
civil rights movement, 20–22
Civil War, 7, 14, 15–16
colorism, 9–10
Congress for Racial Equality, 38

D

discrimination
  addressing, 35–37, 38–39
  covert, 40–41, 49–50
  legal protection against, 23,
    24–25, 26, 27
  racial, 20, 48
  recognizing, 33–34

E

Education Fund of the Texas
    Freedom Network, 29
Equal Employment Opportunity
    Commission, 25, 27, 38
Equal Opportunity Employment
    Act of 1972, 27

F

Fair Housing Act, 26–27
Fifteenth Amendment, 15
Fourteenth Amendment, 15, 17
Freedmen's Bureau, 16
Freedom Rides, 21–22

H

hate speech, 35
Human Genome Project, 4, 11

I

India
  caste sytem in, 10
  racism in, 10

J

Jim Crow laws, 16, 17–18, 29
Johnson, Lyndon, 25

K

Kennedy, John F., 25
King, Martin Luther, Jr., 7,
    20–21, 52

L

Little Rock incident, 18

M

March on Washington, 1963, 21
Martin, Trayvon, 20
microaggressions, 49–52

N

National Association for the Advancement of Colored People (NAACP), 18, 20, 38
nonviolent protest, 21, 22

O

Obama, Barack, 48

P

Parks, Rosa, 20
peer mediation, 35
Plessy v. Ferguson, 17–18

R

racism
  in Africa, 8, 9, 12
  against American Indians, 14
  in Asia, 8–9, 10, 48, 50,
  definition of, 4
  and education, 18, 28, 29–30, 34, 42
  in Europe, 8, 9, 12
  history of, 8–14
  in postracial America, 48–49
  and slavery, 6, 12–13, 14
  in the United States, 6–7, 12–13

racist language
  reporting, 35
  responding to, 33–34
  usage of, 44–45
Ross Initiative in Sports for Equality, 38

S

Scott, Dred, 14
segregation
  de facto, 18
  self, 47
  in the United States, 7, 16–17, 20, 21–22
Shelby County v. Holder, 24
Southern Christian Leadership Conference (SCLC), 20–21
Student Nonviolent Coordinating Committee (SNCC), 21

T

Thirteenth Amendment, 15

V

Voting Rights Act of 1965, 22, 23, 24

W

Walker, Alice, 9

ABOUT THE AUTHOR

Maryellen Lo Bosco began her career with a broad background in the humanities and has branched out into the social sciences and sciences. She writes about literature, history, philosophy, and the life sciences and has taught English language arts in high school and expository writing in college. She also has many years of experience as an academic editor in the social sciences, and in the past decade, she has worked with writers of scholarly books in the field of psychoanalysis. She writes literature guides for both students and teachers and nonfiction books for adolescents. She tutors and teaches students in writing at Suffolk County Community College in Brentwood, New York.

PHOTO CREDITS

Cover Andrew Burton/Getty Images; pp. 4–5 (background) igorstevanovic/Shutterstock.com; p. 5 (inset) Sebastian Kaulitzki/Science Photo Library/Getty Images; pp. 6, 13 MPI/Archive Photos/Getty Images; pp. 8, 15, 23, 33, 40, 48 t81/Shutterstock.com; p. 9 blackwaterimages/E+/Getty Images; p. 10 Jamie McCarthy/Getty Images; p. 17 Afro Newspaper/Gado/Archive Photos/Getty Images; p. 19 Pacific Press/LightRocket/Getty Images; p. 21 Paul Schutzer/The LIFE Picture Collection/Getty Images; p. 26 Robert W. Kelley/The LIFE Picture Collection/Getty Images; p. 28 Mark Makela/Getty Images; p. 30 © AP Images; p. 34 David Schaffer/Caiaimage/Getty Images; p. 36 Klaus Vedfelt/Riser/Getty Images; p. 39 The Boston Globe/Getty Images; p. 41 Caiaimage/Robert Daly/OJO+/Getty Images; p. 43 Jetta Productions/DigitalVision/Getty Images; p. 46 Pictorial Press Ltd/Alamy Stock Photo; p. 49 White House Pool (ISP Pool Images)/Corbis News/Getty Images; p. 51 Patrick Mac Sean/Canopy/Getty Images; p. 52 Mike Kemp/Blend Images/Getty Images.

Design: Michael Moy; Layout: Nicole Russo-Duca; Editor: Carolyn DeCarlo; Photo Research: Nicole Baker